Party Games
for Adults

OTHER BOOKS BY THE SAME AUTHORS

101 Best Games for Teen-Agers
101 Best Games for Girls (6 to 12)
101 Best Action Games for Boys (6 to 12)
101 Best Nature Games & Projects (6 up)
Giant Book of Games
Scrapbook of Real-Life Stories (10 up)
What to Do With Your Preschooler

Party Games for Adults

Icebreakers, Parlor Games, and Party Tips That Will Make Your Guests Flip

BY LILLIAN and GODFREY FRANKEL
with drawings by DOUG ANDERSON

STERLING PUBLISHING CO., INC.
New York

DEDICATED
To Pete

We want to thank many people for helping us write this book—our fellow group workers, recreation leaders and teachers who have recommended games and ideas; those with whom we have played these games; and particularly Sanford Watzman for his able editorial assistance.

Editor's Note
This book was originally published by Sterling Publishing Co., Inc., in 1953. While you'll still find retro inspiration, some of the games have been updated for today's party planners.

Designed by ✑ CREATIVE QUOTIENT - *A Repro Enterprise*

Library of Congress Cataloging-in-Publication Data is available

10 9 8 7 6 5 4 3 2 1

Published by Sterling Publishing Co., Inc.
387 Park Avenue South, New York, NY 10016

© 2007 by Sterling Publishing Co., Inc.

Originally published by Sterling Publishing Co., Inc., in 1953.
Distributed in Canada by Sterling Publishing
c/o Canadian Manda Group, 165 Dufferin Street
Toronto, Ontario, Canada M6K 3H6

Distributed in the United Kingdom by GMC Distribution Services
Castle Place, 166 High Street, Lewes, East Sussex, England BN7 1XU
Distributed in Australia by Capricorn Link (Australia) Pty. Ltd.
P.O. Box 704, Windsor, NSW 2756, Australia

Manufactured in the United States of America
All rights reserved

Sterling ISBN-13: 978-1-4027-4686-4
         ISBN-10: 1-4027-4686-5

For information about custom editions, special sales, premium and corporate purchases, please contact Sterling Special Sales Department at 800-805-5489 or specialsales@sterlingpub.com.

Table of Contents

1. Tips on Playing Games

Increasing interest is being directed toward group games as a natural device for encouraging sociability and for insuring a good time. People lose self-consciousness in a good game. The relaxation of playing games can get individuals better acquainted, provide mutual enjoyment at a party and break down barriers and prejudices.

Toward this end we have tested and selected these *Party Games for Adults*. We hope you have as much fun playing them as we had in selecting them.

When planning games for a party you should be aware of certain essentials. *Here are the most important:*

- Size and type of room for the party.
- Time schedule for playing games.
- Interest, experience and ability of your guests.
- Age and sex distribution (will all or a majority of the guests be male, female, dates, married couples?).
- Sequence of party—what comes before and after games.

Even without experience, most people can lead games. In leading, *you should be aware of the following principles:*

- Read, select and outline the games you want to use, aiming for variety.
- Collect beforehand any material and properties for playing.
- Schedule game-playing at an appropriate time in your program.
- Explain the game clearly and briefly by steps, then demonstrate.

- Begin with an easy game or icebreaker.
- Arrange the game sequence so that games which have the same space arrangement are played together (such as circle games); this keeps reshifting of the group to a minimum.
- Point out mistakes made but *not the players* who make them; encourage the players.
- Arrange for rest periods.
- Try to get the entire group to participate if you think they all want to play.
- Create an atmosphere of warmth, friendliness and informality, and have fun yourself.
- Stop before everyone is played out.
- Don't drag out the program.

Remember that these are games, but more than just play. They should bring enjoyment to every party and make you a success as a host or hostess. Have fun!

2. Icebreakers

NO STRINGS ATTACHED

With just a few pieces of string, you can crack the ice at any party. In this diabolical scheme, the host and hostess stand at the front door, each with a handful of string ends. In welcoming the arrivals, the hostess gives a string-end to each handsome male and the host presents a string-end to each beautiful female.

When everyone has arrived, each guest simultaneously must start to follow the course of the string he holds. He trails it across the floor, over and under chairs and tables, in and out of rooms, and so on, rolling and unknotting it as he goes. In the tangle, he becomes acquainted with most of the guests. Eventually he is startled when he comes face-to-face with a female guest holding the other end of the same untangled string. At this point, host and hostess beam and it becomes evident that they plotted this in advance. Male and female guests thus are paired off for the ensuing festivities.

The hosts, of course, laid the strings out ahead of time, crisscrossing them along the carpets and roping them around obstacles, but always coming to an end at the front door where the other end started. Thus, the host is able to pass out one end of a string while the hostess is passing out the opposite end.

No Strings Attached means that you owe nothing to your hosts for the friendships you make, but some sort of tribute to their cleverness would be in order.

They'll learn each other's names, even if they forget their own.

*Tie them together, and they'll have to get
acquainted quickly.*

VICIOUS CIRCLE

What better way to make sure your guests really get to know each other than to tie them together in a Vicious Circle?

"Alice Brown," you say, "may I introduce Jonathan Applecart?" and you proceed to rope them together. You take a string about five feet long and tie each end loosely around each of Mr. Applecart's wrists. Then, looping a second string of the same length through his tied string (the Vicious Circle) you tie its ends around Miss Brown's wrists.

"Now," you tell them, "separate yourselves without untying the strings or slipping the loops off your wrists."

As newcomers arrive, you tie them up in the same fashion. Soon your living room will look like the snake house at the zoo as arms flail, legs twine in, out and over the strings. The air is filled with cries of, "Hold still, it'll work if I can just get my arm over your head," and "Here, step through this way and I think we've got it!"

But they won't get it that way. Sooner or later one ingenious guest will realize that no amount of twisting and looping will separate two linked circles! If she carries her thinking one step further she will discover the trick: One of the strings must be looped up and pushed under the wrist-loop of the other person, then slipped over the hand—and suddenly you are free! Free to resume the acquaintanceship so auspiciously begun!

SONG SCRAMBLE

This scramble not only gets your guests acquainted rapidly, but it also brings out any latent vocal talent they have and organizes them into, of all things, competing choral groups. All the singing is so spontaneous that even the confirmed shower soloist will find herself joining in.

The host or hostess needs only a pencil and a scratch pad. He writes out several songs, line by line, but jots down only one line on each slip of paper. Then he shuffles the papers like a deck of cards and deals them out just after all the guests have arrived.

One guest will receive, for example, "O give me a home," another will get "Gave truth to the night" a third "Where the skies are cloudy all day," and a fourth "For the Land of the Free." The fun begins when the guests enter into a mad scramble to find the holders of all the slips that will complete their song.

As soon as a group assembles correctly, it can begin to sing the song. The first group to do this is the winner.

Easy? You'll be surprised how unfamiliar a well-known song can look when all you see is an isolated line. Occasionally, at least one line will be missing when the rest are in—and you have to find the guest who is holding it. Some lyrics are certain to get so scrambled in the ensuing anxiety that even their composers won't recognize them.

For a variation, you can substitute proverbs or familiar quotations for songs, and they may be recited instead of sung.

MULTIPLICATION DANCE

Sometimes referred to as the "Conscription Dance," this game succeeds in drafting the party slackers known as wallflowers. Unless your house has secret panels, or unless the bashful ones are so camouflaged that they appear as part of the wallpaper, there will be no escape for them.

The dance begins with only one couple. They perform for their audience until the music is stopped—play the music not more than one minute. Then each of them pulls a wallflower from the wall and dances with him or her. Now two couples are dancing. The next time the music is stopped, four more slackers are dragged to the front. This means four couples are dancing and soon there will be eight.

When *everybody* is dancing, the person who had been stopping the music can cease. He has done his duty. No one will notice, because everybody is now acquainted with everybody else.

WHAT'S YOUR LINE?

For introducing guests to each other in a memorable way, the clever hostess will play What's Your Line?, and subtly demonstrate that all her "strangers" have many things in common. She will put on the witness stand, as it were, each guest in turn.

Please be seated. Now, Miss Vanderveer, act out your vocation—in pantomime.

Miss Vanderveer dons her hat and coat, pulling her hat down over her eyes and wrapping her head in her coat collar. Then she simulates typewriting while gazing furtively to right and left. Several guesses from the guests. Correct answer: She's a crime novelist.

Next comes a doctor (using a stethoscope) or an automobile salesman (opening and closing car doors) and so on.

FACE TO FACE

To get everybody acquainted at your party, one good way is to come face to face with your problem. Face to Face is a game with several aliases: Back to Back, Side to Side, Toe to Toe, Elbow to Elbow, etc.

The aliases more or less explain the action. Everybody chooses a partner, but one player (usually the host or hostess) has none. The hostess calls out commands, which the partners obey literally. For example, "Side by side!" means the partners must stand side by side. After a few such commands as "Fingernail to Fingernail!" and "Eyebrow to Eyebrow," the hostess cries: "All change!" Then, each player, including the host, scurries to find a new partner, and the player left without one becomes "It."

One advantage of this game is that each guest gets to view every other guest from all possible angles. After playing Face to Face, none of the guests is likely to forget a face.

LIVING STATUES

No host ever had a guest list like this: Napoleon, Cupid, Mercury, Rodin's Thinker, George Washington (crossing the Delaware) and the patriots in the Spirit of '76. With these Very Important People and many more, your parties will be the talk of the town.

Here's the way to turn your guests into VIPs and have fun in the process.

Write down beforehand the names of well-known statues, key figures in famous paintings, easily caricatured movie stars, and athletic figures (such as a basketball player, figure skater, wrestler and baseball umpire).

Divide your guests into two equal teams. All the members of one team take slips simultaneously from a box. Each assumes his assigned pose and holds it like a statue while members of the opposite team try to identify him. If they succeed they get one point for each correct identification. Otherwise, the posing team gets the point. The hostess, who does not participate, acts as judge of whether the statue was enacted correctly.

The teams alternate and each gets at least two chances to pose. By this time, all your guests will be thoroughly acquainted.

PROFILES

For all you know, you may have a Jay Leno, a "Great Profile," among you, who will become famous after a game of Profiles.

See him now? He's the first guest to arrive at the party. As he enters there is a spotlight lamp shining on one side of his face, and the hostess draws a profile from the shadow cast on the wall. (The hostess, of course, has a big cardboard and a number of sheets of 5 x 7 paper set aside beforehand.) As the guests arrive, the hostess gives each the same treatment in turn. No one is allowed to peek at the profiles that the hostess is drawing.

After completing each "portrait" the hostess writes a number on the front and the name of the person on the back. Then she posts the sketches or lays them out on the floor.

The guests then try to identify the profiles. Is there a Leno (or a Barbra Streisand) in the house? Profiles such as those make the game easier. The guest who identifies the greatest number of sketches is the winner.

DANCE WITH THE BROOMSTICK

The best way to draw a wallflower toward the center of the room is to hand him a broomstick to dance with. Without discovering the underlying psychological reason for this addiction to broomsticks, you can be sure that the trick always works. For icebreaking purposes, each guest may be properly deemed a wallflower.

The host or hostess plays a piano or phonograph, after pairing off the guests at random. Each person is given another person to dance with, except one, who is paired with the broomstick. When the music is suddenly stopped, everyone must hurry to change partners. Naturally, the guest with the broomstick displays the greatest desire to change. In the end, someone always ends up with the broomstick.

After enough guests have danced with the broomstick (and are only too happy to dance with a human thereafter) the real party can begin.

LAST COUPLE STOOP

This game stoops to a new low in party pastimes and manages to reach a new high in hilarity whenever it's played.

Each male chooses a female partner, and remembers what she looks like. Then the guests form two circles, men on the inside women on the outside. The host or hostess attends a CD player or radio. As the music starts, males walk clockwise and females counter-clockwise. The music stops suddenly. Now is the time for all good men to come to the aid of their partners. They rush around, find each other, hold hands and stoop. The last couple to stoop is eliminated. The game goes on as before.

There are times when the immediate area may become so crowded that there is hardly room to stoop, much less to hold hands, and everybody gets bumped in the traffic jam.

The couple eliminated from each round gets revenge by becoming "referee" and helping spot the next "last couple."

3. Parlor Games

GIANT JIGSAW PUZZLE

In this game, the host or hostess puts advertisements to work and makes up a giant puzzle. First she clips from old magazines the illustrations accompanying about ten well-known ads. Then she mounts the pictures on cardboard or heavy paper, after which she cuts each picture into four or more irregular pieces.

As she numbers the face of each piece at random from 1 to 40 (or higher), she keeps a record of the combinations that comprise a complete picture. Now she shuffles the pieces, mixing them thoroughly, and places them on a table.

Guests, gather round! See the pretty pictures? Yes, it looks like modern art. You're not supposed to touch the pieces. Just write down in groups the numbers of those pieces that you think came from the same ad.

First person to submit a completely correct list, or the player with the largest percentage correct, wins the game and can take home the pieces. The hostess acts as judge.

PHOTO GUESS

Best for a group in which everyone knows everyone else intimately, this game requires your guests to bring with them to the party one of their childhood photos. Host and hostess throw their own in, too.

The host collects the pictures from the guests as they arrive. Then he prepares an identifying record of all the photographs and numbers them on the back. When he finishes and lines them up in rows on a table or on the floor, the guessing begins. With pencil and paper in hand, the guests scan the Rogues' Gallery and write down the names and photo numbers as they guess.

You are in for an awful jolt if you believe you can identify 100 percent of the pictures. Here's a hint: skulls change very little as people grow older, yet faces, as recorded on photos, often appear quite different. In most cases, of course, the change is not complete and your guests will find it fun (if not gruesome) to see what has happened to their features down through the years. You'll hear close friends say: "Why that couldn't be John. He's so rugged today and he was such a delicate child!" or "Why don't you revert to pigtails? You were such a cute little girl!"

Innocent faces may fool you ... and your side has only two chances to guess.

UP JENKINS!

Legend has it that this game originated with a group of Mississippi riverboat gamblers. They grew tired of the constant admonition "Keep your hands above the table," and so they invented a game that legitimized the sly passage of a coin.

"Up Jenkins!" requires a long table with two teams sitting opposite each other. One team has possession of a coin that can be passed surreptitiously from palm to palm under the table until, suddenly, the captain of the opposing team cries: "Up Jenkins!"

At this command, all the members of the team with the coin must obey by raising their hands above their heads, fists clenched. The coin, of course, is concealed in one of the fists. As the opposing captain gives the second command, "Down Jenkins!" all members of the coin-holding team must slap their palms down flat on the table.

Naturally, the sound of a coin hitting the table will be heard, but who has the coin? The challenging team gets two chances to guess. Usually the players consult before one challenger (one of the two nearest the captain) points to a player and says: "Show up!" The player thus challenged must raise his hands. If he hasn't the coin, the second challenge is given.

If the challenging team has guessed right, it scores a point and gets possession of the coin for the next round. If it fails to guess correctly, the other team gets a point and keeps the coin for another round. And so on, until one team gets 10 points.

Who was Jenkins? Possibly a Mississippi gambler with chewing gum on his palms.

FRUIT BASKET

(Note: This game has the approval of the ARWSCSB—the Amalgamated Riders Without Seats on Crowded Subway and Buses of the NACM—the National Association of Chair Manufacturers.)

Lull your guests into a feeling of false security by seating them in chairs to start with. Arrange the chairs in a circle. "It" (the host or hostess) is the only person not seated. Assign the following names to your guests: apple, orange, pear, tangerine, and so forth, using the names of fruits only. In large groups, more than one player may have the same assigned name.

Now the fun begins: "It" says: "Apple(s) change places with orange(s)" or "Tangerines, pears, pineapples and plums change places!" At the command, the players named scramble for each other's places. None may remain seated if her appellation is called. "It" joins in the rush and tries to commandeer one of the seats. If she succeeds, she becomes the fruit of the player left unseated and the latter becomes the new "It." Otherwise, "It" must try again.

In desperation, when "It" is foiled time and again, she may give the general command: "Fruit basket upset!" Then *everybody* must get up and change seats!

Don't use any rickety furniture.

LEMON TWIST

This is not a game with used cars, but with real lemons. You can get nowhere fast, when driving a lemon.

Divide your guests into two or more equal teams. Give the leader of each team a full-length pencil and a full-grown lemon. As the teams line up single file, mark a starting line and a finish line along the floor (about 20 feet away at most).

The object of the game is to push the lemon with the pencil along the floor in a straight line—if you can! Each player must push it to the finish line and back to the next teammate in line. The team to finish first wins.

What you discover is that the lemon always keeps rolling, despite a slight wobble. You'll have difficulty keeping to your lane, so be sure the furniture is pushed back. Here's a hint from experienced lemon rollers: don't push too fast as this generally causes the lemon to roll the wrong way.

RUMOR

Want to hear gossip? Instead of just sitting around and waiting for it to start, why not garble it properly? Divide your guests into two teams and appoint for each team a leader, who immediately consults with you (the host or hostess).

"What do you want to talk about?" you ask.

One team leader may say, "I'm not a rumor monger, but I understand Agnes's husband got a raise and bought her a mink coat."

"Let's put that in writing," you say.

So each leader writes down on a card this identical sentence: "Agnes's husband got a raise; that's why she has that mink coat."

Now the Rumor really begins. The leaders return to the heads of their lines, turn around and say to the next players: "Agnes's husband ... etc. Pass it on!"

The second player then passes the spoken intelligence to the third and so on down the line. (A long line is best.) When it gets to the last players, the host asks them each to say aloud what they have heard.

One may have heard: "Agnes's brother got a loan and bought a mink farm; Agnes skinned the mink herself;" while the other may come up with: "Alice's pet mink died of an overdose of sleeping pills, and someone was arrested for murder."

The host then asks the leaders to read the written messages they started with. When the laughter dies down, the second players move to the heads of the line, choose some new Rumor, and everyone tries again. Do this until each person has had a chance to start a Rumor. After playing that long, your guests will probably be convinced for life of the dangers of repeating gossip.

RHYTHM

Some people "ain't got rhythm." This can be remedied by playing this game, which may keep your guests speaking in cadence for the next three days.

All gather in a circle and begin a 1-2-3-4 beat by counting and clapping hands three times, then holding their hands outstretched (as in Pat-a-Cake) on the 4-beat. On this beat, you don't count out loud either but listen as the player whose turn it is calls out a word like "good." Then the rhythm continues with 1-2-3-4. On the next 4-beat, the next player in the circle must call out a word that is either a synonym, antonym, or a word with a close association to the previous word, "good" in this case.

The second player may not repeat the word, so let's suppose he says "bad" (the antonym). Then the next player on the 4-beat may say neither "bad" nor "good" but may say "dog," which is his association with "bad." Or he could have said "worse" or "better" or "gangster" or any associated word except the name of a person or place. The calling of the word on the 4-beat must be fast enough to keep up the rhythm.

As the rhythm gets faster, more and more of the players will falter. Those who falter, miss or give a wrong word are eliminated. There's no time here to finger a dictionary—even one with a thumb index.

MURDER

"Murder" will bring life to your party. Like this pun, the game itself should be funny and amateurish. Therefore, you should invite guests without previous experience as either killers, detectives or corpses.

For the serious business of Murder, put into a hat as many slips of paper as you have guests.

One slip will say "killer" and another "detective," but all the others will be blank. The player who draws the "detective" slip announces herself, takes a seat at the far end of the room and stays there. The player who draws the "killer" slip keeps it absolutely secret. The lights go out.

Since nobody knows the identity of the killer, everybody is on the move to get away from him. Meanwhile, the "killer" stalks one of the guests. At a ripe moment he "kills" him or her by throwing a "headlock." The corpse slumps to the floor. Everybody keeps moving until someone discovers the corpse. The lights go on. Each player stands where she is.

The detective goes to work. At the scene of the crime, she observes the corpse and searches for clues, if there are any. Motive? Is the corpse somebody's mother-in-law? Suicide? (No-o, that's against the rules.) Then who did it? It's the detective's job to find out.

The detective calls for a searchlight (a flashlight with normally weak batteries will do) and, one by one, turns it on the face of everybody present.

Did you see the killing? (No, it was too dark.) Then why are you so close to the corpse? (I happened to be walking this way! Is there a law against walking?) Do you have a police record? Any traffic offenses? (I refuse to answer on the grounds that it may incriminate me.) Those being questioned must answer *all relevant queries* truthfully. When the killer is questioned, he may lie (well, little white lies) as he sees fit.

Whether the case is solved or unsolved, after a certain length of time the "case" ends. The slips of paper are returned to the hat and a new killer and detective are chosen. This continues until you have a crime wave.

SCRAMBLED ANATOMY

One of the first things a baby learns is to identify the various parts of his anatomy. The mark of maturity is to be able to do this with a changed set of words—calling an ear a nose, and a nose an ear. Party guests are forever amused to find that many of their number don't know their hip from their elbow.

To begin the game, "It" approaches a guest and, touching her own thumb (for example) says: "This is my toe."

Before "It" can complete a brief count of 5 (to himself), the guest addressed must counter by touching his toe and replying: "This is my thumb." If the player flunks this impromptu exam, he becomes "It" and approaches another guest.

Pointing to his eye, the new "It" may now say: "This is my tooth."

The correct answer to this is to point to your tooth and say: "This is my eye." Sounds simple. Anybody can do this. Just try it.

Rattles may be passed out to the consistent losers.

FIND THE RING

This is an adaptation of the old "shell game" in which your fists are used in lieu of shells and a ring is substituted for the pea. In the house party version, all the guests are permitted to get in on the act.

First, get a string just long enough to make a circle around everyone present. The string is then passed through the loop of the ring and the ends of the string are tied together. The guests in the circle each hold onto the string with their fists in front of them.

As "It" (usually host or hostess to start) watches from the center of the circle, the players slide their fists back and forth over the string, passing the ring from one to another at the same time. "It" stops the action whenever he chooses and then must guess who has the ring. A correct guess means he joins the circle and the player discovered with the ring becomes "It."

With really deceptive players, "It" can have a very difficult detective task.

GRAB THE PLATE

In cartoons a hungry thief always happens along as soon as an oven-fresh pie is placed on the windowsill to cool. Good-bye pie! Pity the thief, eating up all those calories, and think how slim you'll stay when you play Grab the Plate. In this game you don't have your pie, and you don't eat it too.

The guests sit in a circle around an empty pie tin. "It" leaves her chair and goes into the center of the circle. She takes the tin pie plate and spins it on edge on the floor. As soon as the plate begins to spin, she calls out the name of another player and dashes to her own chair. The player called rushes to the plate and picks it up. If he fails to pick it up before "It" is seated, he becomes the new "It" as the game continues.

Scoring will add fun to Grab the Plate. Award one point to each player who gets to the plate in time.

BALLOON FOOTBALL

A survey taken at a New Year's Eve party showed that most of the guests didn't even notice the balloons used for decoration. But when the balloons were used as part of the program, they took on added dignity and importance. When the host and hostess organized a game of Balloon Football, the result was not only a vindication of the balloons but also of the party.

To play Balloon Football, divide the guests into equal teams and station a "goalie" at each end of the room for each team. The goalie, armed with a straight pin, must stand on a chair. His job is to puncture the balloon that his team pushes or bats toward him. When he pops a balloon, he scores a point for his team. The players (who may wear earplugs if they wish) are at all times occupied with two balloons, as each team has one.

While a team is trying to push its balloon toward its goalie, it must also keep the other balloon from reaching the opposing goalie. In passing, you are permitted only to tip the balloon to another player, not to hold it or let it touch the floor.

The hostess should prepare an abundance of balloons, as they may become as expendable as baseballs at a World Series game.

BLACK MAGIC

An international conference of witch doctors, convening recently on the lost continent, passed a resolution that only four words—*black, white, yes* and *no*—are to be considered official Black Magic words. In the American version of the game of Black Magic, a leader or "voodoo artist" is selected. It is her job to trick the other guests into saying one of the Black Magic words. Anybody so duped is banished from the game, which continues until only one player remains. He becomes the "voodoo artist" for the next round.

The leader may use any verbal device at her command in trying to elicit a fatal answer from the other players. Time is on her side because, as she fires questions at the guests, they must answer without delay. The leader may be nonchalantly telling a story and interrupt suddenly to ask of a player, "Is that right?" A "yes" or "no" means out. Or: "Isn't your name Paula?" Or: "What's the color of milk?"

Each guest must answer *immediately* when asked a question. He tries not to use the words, "black," "white," "yes" and "no," and his answers needn't make sense. However, he must accept the embarrassing responsibility for his statement, which is usually more nonsensical and hilarious than the question that preceded it.

No, yes?

WORD HUNT

Word Hunt is a game especially suited for a housewarming party. It will acquaint your guests with every nook and cranny in your home. Besides, during your advance preparation—fun in itself—you may even locate Dad's missing cuff link or that favorite CD you'd mislaid!

Start playing Word Hunt by giving each guest or couple a number. Then tell them that you've hidden a number of cards, about two inches by four, in various places about the house. Each card has a letter of the alphabet on one side and on the reverse side a number corresponding to one of the guests' numbers.

Each guest or couple will find a total of six cards bearing their number. If they come across a card belonging to someone else, they return it to its hiding place without telling anyone where it is. When a player or couple has found all six cards, they arrange the letters to form a word. Whoever is the first to assemble the word is the winner.

Since your guests are likely to search in the least obvious places, better make sure that Junior has removed his frogs and hamsters temporarily.

PARSON JACK

Why do people come home from an auction so dissatisfied? They may have called too high a figure and bought something they didn't even want. Or else they bid too low a figure, or accidentally repeated somebody else's offer, and failed to buy something they did want. A good game of Parson Jack will whip you into shape for any auction.

Parson Jack is the host. He is No. 1 and the others are numbered consecutively. They are seated in a circle with No. 2 at the host's right and the last player at his left. The host starts the game by saying:

> Parson Jack, Parson Jack,
> Some say white, some say black,
> But I say—

He calls the number of any player and immediately counts from 1 to 10. Within that time, the designated player must call the number of another person. If she doesn't, or if she mistakenly calls her own number or a number not in the game, she takes the seat to the Parson's left. Everybody else moves up one, and the players are renumbered so that the sequence of numbers is unbroken. When the designated player does answer correctly and in time, she in turn calls another number and counts to 10.

The game continues, with a reshuffling of players each time someone falters. Since the object of the game is to unseat the Parson by making HIM falter, his number, No. 1, is the most popular number in the game!

"Going, going, gone? Why, see here, Mr. Auctioneer, I *am* Parson Jack!"

PING PONG BREEZE

Here is a "Look, Ma, no hands!" game without a bike. Anybody who uses hands is disqualified, but actually you don't need hands—you'll be surprised how far a Ping Pong ball will roll when you just puff at it.

Begin by moving the furniture out of the way and dividing your guests into two teams. Then mark off with string a playing area about 20 feet long and 6 feet wide. Goals for each team are the opposite ends of the 20-foot playing space. Place the Ping Pong ball in the center. Now both teams begin puffing at the ball at the same time.

The idea is to blow the ball across the goal line for your team. If the ball goes out-of-bounds, it is placed back in the middle of the playing area at the line where it went out, as in football. A point is scored each time a team blows the ball over its goal line, and five points clinch the game.

If your breeze capacity isn't up to par, you may just want to pass the ball to "windier" players on your team. Anyone who feels too dignified to get down on hands and knees to play this game may be taken care of with one of the Ping Pong paddles.

MY PAST

Going to Hollywood? Supply your guests with paper and pencil and they'll supply you with a truckload of scenarios to take along with you.

The players write fragments of a story as you give them a series of commands in a sequence such as the following: Write a boy's name with brief description; girl's name, ditto; where they met; how they met; his first words to her; her reply; what happened next; the comment from neighbors; and the consequences.

After each command, the guests write down the installment, fold over the paper to hide what they've written and pass the paper to their left. The next command is given and the process is repeated.

There should be as many commands as there are guests. When the papers have been passed for the last time, they take turns reading the stories. Each guest joins the phrases and supplies his own continuity.

CAMOUFLAGE

Before your guests arrive, place a large number of small objects around the room. Don't hide them. Leave them out in the open, only make them inconspicuous by placing them on or near objects of similar color.

For example, a blue button can be placed on a blue chair, a brown leaf on a brown carpet, a green postage stamp on a green plant, salt on a white cloth, etc., even a transparent piece of Scotch Tape stuck to the leg of a chair.

Make lists of these objects for each guest and yourself. On your own, note where you've placed the objects. When your guests are ready to play give them each a list and a pencil and let them go to it. They walk singly (or preferably in couples), trying to find these "hidden" objects. They write down their discoveries *without* pointing to the objects or letting on that they have seen them.

Time limit should be about 15 minutes. When the time is up the winner is the player or couple who has found the most objects.

BOTTLE BUILD-UP

The toothpick and the match come about as close as anything else to being disruptive influences in our society. People are always asking for matches, always take more toothpicks than they need. Bottle Build-Up teaches people to *get rid* of toothpicks and matches, instead of acquiring them.

Set up an empty, narrow-necked bottle before your guests and give each of them a quantity of toothpicks or wooden matches (40 each if there are less than 10 in your group and 20 each if there are more than 10 guests). The object is to stack the matches or toothpicks on the top of the bottle, across the opening. Guest No. 1 places one of his matches there; Guest No. 2 places a match beside it. This continues, the guests proceeding in turn, until one of them, in trying to add to the pile, upsets it. He must add all the fallen matches to what is left of his initial allotment, and the game goes on. The Winner is the first player to get rid of all his matches.

In an illegal variation of the game, the players must pay for their matches or their toothpicks. For each match knocked off the bottle, the player who is guilty pays a penny. The interior of the bottle becomes a jackpot for the coins, winner takes all.

TILLIE WILLIAMS

Everyone loves Tillie Williams, even though her best friends admit she's a little odd. In fact, the hostess said, "Tillie Williams is odd, but not crazy."

Her husband, no mean gossip himself, added, "She's silly, but not stupid."

"Tillie loves coffee but hates tea," the hostess mentioned.

"Yes," said the host, "she loves bees but not honey."

It becomes more and more mystifying as the two of them gab on and on about Tillie Williams. Suddenly a clever guest catches on. He chimes in with, "She wears boots, but not galoshes."

One by one the other guests "get wise" and contribute juicy little tidbits of their own—all about Tillie Williams' likes and dislikes. "She likes wool but not silk," says one. "She loves Tennessee but hates Kentucky."

Getting impatient? Well, by this time you should have surmised that Tillie Williams (note the double "l" in each monicker!) likes everything spelled with *double letters*. Tillie's really funny, see?

4. Mental Games

GUESS THE AUTHORS

Who said: "The British are coming!"? (Correct answer: Paul Revere. Incorrect: Ed Sullivan.)

"Read my Lips." Correct: George H.W. Bush. Incorrect: Milli Vanilli.

"I'm a wild and crazy guy!" True speaker: Steve Martin. Never said it: Bill Gates.

Such a list of choice quotations is prepared by the host or hostess in advance of the party. After the guests are divided into two teams, the host fires the quotations at them. Each team may gather in a huddle with pencil and paper, but must come up with one answer written.

The party-giver may consult a book of familiar quotations or the Internet in preparing the questions. His list should include change-of-pace sayings like known "catchphrases" of party guests. Everyone is an author in this democratic game.

TEAKETTLE

Because the English language has so many homonyms (words that sound alike but have different meanings), an educational campaign to simplify the language is now under way. In this campaign, the word Teakettle is substituted for all homonyms.

One person starts by leaving the room. By the time "It" returns, the other players have agreed upon a pair of homonyms (in this example, "write" and "right") and each of them has thought of a different sentence using both words together. The sentences need not make much sense, as:

"I teakettled all teakettle cookies."

"I will teakettle a letter with my teakettle hand."

Of course, as "It" is told the sentences, she is supposed to guess the words that have been so aptly replaced by Teakettle. In a gathering of large size (20 or so), she should be given one guess for each person. When fewer are playing, "It" should be given more guesses accordingly. As soon as she guesses, the player who gave the last clue becomes "It" and gets teakettled in the same manner.

Pencils, paper, a little head-scratching ... and one player who needs a calculator.

HIDDEN WORDS

As you well know, a better understanding and appreciation of literature comes from reading "between the lines." To this we might add the following bit of advice: "Read *into* the words and find what other words are hidden there." This game will do nothing to increase your reading speed, but it may help your spelling.

You can play all evening with one word. The host chooses it and announces it to everyone, after seeing that all the guests are supplied with pencil and pad. Let's say the word is "automobile." You may write down whatever words can be made (three letters or more) out of the letters in this word. You might find "lot," "but," "mob," etc.

Then—and this will test your knowledge even more—you may also name objects and people ordinarily found in the general word, in this case "automobile." You might name the "driver," "carburetor," "radiator" and so on. Now, after writing these down, you can also analyze them. Out of "driver," you will get words such as "dive," "rid," "river," etc. Out of "carburetor," you may get "arc," "tear," and so on.

Set a time limit of about 15 minutes, if you want. The winner is the player who writes down the longest list of words.

TEST YOUR MEMORY

Why is it so difficult to remember what we have just seen? Is it that our memory is at fault? Or aren't we observant? Perhaps we just don't make use of our natural abilities. Here is a game to test your observation and memory.

The hostess must prepare a table in advance of the party with such objects scattered on it as a pencil, hat, carrot, dish, pin, ribbon, bracelet, ring, spool of thread, cigar, magazine, clip, eraser, sock, bottle, photograph, trophy, cellphone, shoelace, razor blade, tablecloth, pear, coin and book.

The guests each get a piece of paper and pencil, and are allowed no more than 60 seconds to look at the objects. They may not write down what they see, but must wait until the hostess covers the objects with a cloth (or asks the guests to turn their backs). Then the players are supposed to remember every object and write them down in a list.

The player who writes the longest correct list is the winner. Don't be surprised if the winner has only a 50% or 60% score.

GHOSTS AND SUPER GHOSTS

Since the days of Macbeth, the game of Ghosts has started with one letter of the alphabet. One player in the crowd recites this letter and you're off to a ghostly start. If the letter was "T," for example, the second player may add "R," with "travel" in mind. The next player follows suit, and the next, each adding letters until a word is about to be completed, and each striving not to end a word herself. The person forced to complete the word becomes one-third of a ghost. (Three-thirds and you disappear.)

A quick-witted player will not tack the "L" on the end of "travel" but will add "S" with thought of "travesty," thus dooming another of the players. The quick switch is what has made Ghosts a universal favorite through the ages. Is there an adult who hasn't played the simple version of Ghosts?

Today, everyone is playing Super Ghosts or Double Ghosts. Unlike its parent game, this starts with two letters and you may add on one letter at a time from either side. For instance, you might start with "UD" and add an "A" in front or "I" on the end, with the word "audible" in mind. A player faced with "audibl" will not add the "E" but will put an "N" at the beginning to switch to "inaudible." Switch when you're stuck and be prepared with plenty of prefixes and suffixes!

Many more challenges are given in Super Ghosts. You will wonder many times what a player has in mind, and if you think he's bluffing, you may challenge him to reveal his word. If the word he has in mind actually can be constructed that way, the challenger becomes one-third of a ghost. But should the bluff be a bluff, or should the challenged player be misspelling the word in mind, then the latter becomes one-third. Proper nouns are not allowed. Naturally, the last person left in the game is the winner.

Some tough nuts to crack for a starting pair are "YP," "HG," and "RQ."

BOTTICELLI

In playing this game, none of the participants should claim to be Botticelli, even if they know that artist. Better-known appellations should be picked, such as Einstein, Jennifer Aniston/Bob Dylan, Shaquille O'Neal/Stephen King, Julius Caesar and others.

"It" will say: "I am a person whose last name begins with C," if he is thinking of Julius Caesar. Then the others have a chance to ask him questions about "C's" work in order to discover his identity.

For instance, a player may ask: "Are you a musician?"

"It's" answer should be: "No, I am not Chopin."

Or: "Are you a statesman?" to which the answer is "No, I am not Churchill."

If someone should ask: "Are you a hockey player?" and "It" cannot answer with the name of a hockey player beginning with C, then the player who stumped him has the right to ask a more specific question. He might then ask: "Are you living?" or "Are you an American?" to which "It" must answer "yes" or "no" truthfully.

The game continues until someone guesses that C stands for "Caesar." The guesser then becomes "It" for a round and offers another mystery letter—anything but B for Botticelli.

TOSS THE PROVERB

When you stub your toe, do you say: "It's no use crying over spilt milk?"

When Junior has cut dolls out of the curtains, do you mutter "Every cloud has a silver lining?"

While trying to live with a toothache, do you remark: "Necessity is the mother of invention," when you mean "Any port in a storm?"

To be able to conjure up the right saying at the right time requires a bit of training. If you have trouble, you should learn to play Toss the Proverb. When the players are seated, one player tosses a small empty box or a ball to another player. The receiver must recite a proverb—any proverb—before the thrower counts slowly to 10. If she fails to quote one or if she quotes one that has been used before, she drops out of the game. She returns the object to the thrower who then throws it to another player. In the later rounds, thinking of a proverb is not so easy.

If you have one player noting down on paper the proverbs that are quoted, you can then switch to "Highbrow Proverbs," which involves butchering the beautiful simplicity of our proverbs by recasting them.

For example, "Absence makes the heart grow fonder" may be rephrased: "A lack of appearance can cause a muscle of the circulatory system to pump with greater affection." "A stitch in time saves nine" becomes "A simple movement with a steel object may eliminate as many as the digit before ten."

AVOID THAT LETTER

Too often the conversation at parties gets into a rut. Conscientious hostesses can avoid the situation by selecting a letter of the alphabet and forbidding her guests to use it. At the same time, she tries to *force* them to use it. Here are the results, if the letter she chooses is "Q":

HOSTESS (*to John*): What does a duck say?

JOHN: He makes a sound that no other fowl can make.

HOSTESS (*to Elaine*): How does that go—"All What on the Western Front"?

ELAINE: Well, although not quoting the title directly, you could say it is "All Tranquil ..."

HOSTESS: That's two points against you!

ELAINE: What did I say?

HOSTESS: You said Quoting and tranQuil.

ELAINE: I should have been "All Quiet ..."

The hostess asks each of her guests one question. Those who become ensnared are assessed one point for each use of the forbidden letter. (A scorekeeper keeps track.) Another guest chooses another letter and proceeds to question the others. After all have had a turn at banishing a letter from the language, the points are totalled and the winner is the guest with the lowest total.

When common consonants and vowels are the letters to be avoided, you can pile up points by the dozen. Imagine a sentence without an "E."

DILEMMA

It's a normal evening at home. You're watching *Grey's Anatomy*, but your boyfriend wants to watch *CSI*. What do you do? Don't bother to answer—we're only posing a dilemma. In this game, the dilemma is more important than the solution.

Now assume you are playing a game. Two guests, selected at random, have left the room. While they're gone, the rest of you have thought of the above dilemma. The guests return and must try to discover your dilemma. They do this by posing *other* dilemmas and gauging your answers to their questions. Here we go:

THE TWO GUESTS: Your car is stalled on the streetcar tracks. What would you do?

THE REST OF YOU *(answering the question as if it concerned the TV dilemma)*: I'd tell him he saw it last week.

GUESTS: Your boyfriend says it's time for the show to start and you still aren't dressed. What would you do?

YOU: I'd tell him to take out the trash.

The two guests work against a time limit of, say, five minutes. Sometimes the answers are revealing. In the first question the answer provided a clue—"I'd tell *him*..." The second (regarding the "trash") gave no noticeable information and might have been misleading. Before the time is up, the dilemma must be discovered. But guess or not, the two guests join the others after the time is up, and two more guests leave the room. The game continues as a new dilemma is conceived.

GUGGENHEIM

Guggenheim say: "Do not be fooled by apparent simplicity of Guggenheim. Guggenheim is easy to play, difficult to win."

When your guests are to play Guggenheim, give them each pencil and paper on which you have already copied the framework of the accompanying model on the opposite page (or something similar). Leave blanks for each item except the column headings (Animal, etc.) and the word you are going to use (in this case, Hospital).

The guests get three minutes to fill in the blanks, without collaboration. As the model shows, the first animal, city, etc., must be aligned with the first letter of the Guggenheim word and must begin with that letter. And so, down the line in the same fashion.

Players who choose obvious answers, such as those given in the model, are *not* likely to win. The idea is to get unique items and places to fill in the spaces—but you may not consult dictionaries, atlases, the Internet, or books of any kind.

The score is figured this way: Let's say you have 15 participants. The maximum for each space then is 15 points and these are awarded to the player who wrote an item no one else used. If five players chose the same word, or if five players chose different words that no one else used, each will get 3 points. When the same word appears on all 15 papers, each player gets just 1 point. The highest number of points wins. Hint: choose a good mathematician to compute the scores.

For a super game, choose words with double letters like Guggenheim and Bookkeeper, and use more column headings, such as Vegetable, Mineral, State, Nation, Athlete, Actor, Politician.

	Animal	City	Flower	Food
H	Hamster	Hartford	Honeysuckle	Ham
O	Ostrich	Oklahoma City	Orchid	Orange
S	Steer	Seattle	Sweet Pea	Sausage
P	Pig	Pittsburgh	Petunia	Pork
I	Iguana	Indianapolis	Iris	Ice Cream
T	Tiger	Toledo	Tulip	Tongue
A	Alligator	Annapolis	Apple Blossom	Apricot
L	Leopard	Louisville	Lily	Lentil

WHY, WHEN, WHERE?

Reporters are remarkable people. Besides being sleuths who solve crimes on television, they can learn almost anything by asking, "When? Why? Where?" Try it and see!

Let one person leave the room while the others decide on a noun for him to guess, e.g., "pencil." When the player ("It") returns, he proceeds with the following journalistic-style interview:

Q.: WHEN do you like it?

A.: Almost anytime.

Q.: WHY do you like it?

A.: It makes life easier.

Q.: WHERE do you like it?

A.: On paper.

"It" continues asking the same questions but always gets new answers. When he guesses the noun, or if he gives up (don't tell his city editor), someone else leaves the room and a new noun is decided upon.

THE MIND READER

At a party the hostess remarked, quite casually, that she had predicted the re-election of Bush in 2004. How? She had read the minds of the voters. The guests became interested. Could she read their minds—now? The hostess replied that certainly she could read their minds.

She gives each of them a small square of paper of identical size. After the guests write down a word or phrase, they each fold the papers twice in half and hand them to the host. He collects them in a pile and hands them, closed and folded, to the Mind Reader.

The hostess takes the folded paper at the top of the pile, holds it pressed to her forehead, closes her eyes and chants the "magic" words: "Ectoderm, endoderm, oyster, crab. Crayfish, starfish, zoology, lab." Thus given strength, she quotes the word from the folded paper: "Cat."

"Why," says the host, "that's exactly what I wrote—'cat.' How does she do it?"

The Mind Reader takes her hand from her forehead, unfolds the paper and reads it. "Yes, 'cat' it was," she says, checking her answer.

Actually, the Mind Reader had a confederate (the host) who by previous arrangement wrote down "cat" and put his paper at the **bottom** of the stack when he turned the papers over to the Mind Reader. When the Mind Reader "checked" on her first answer, she was really reading the contents of the top paper, which everybody thought contained "cat." It said "rain"—as the "cat" paper was at the bottom of the pile. So she unhesitatingly holds the folded paper to her forehead, chants the magic words and says: "Rain!"

"Why," says the person who wrote "rain," "that's exactly what I wrote." Then the Mind Reader "checks" again and finds out what the next word is.

This operation, with the Mind Reader always one jump ahead of the guests, continues until all the words and messages have been quoted. Will the guests catch on? If you and your confederate work together smoothly, their chances of catching on are fifty-fifty.

HINK PINK

Hink Pink, in the Zwatacarmody language, is the imperative form of the verb "to think." Literally translated, it means: "Think! Think! This is what you have to do when you play Hink Pink."

One player will start by saying: "I have a hink pink." What he means is that he is thinking of an object that can be described in two rhyming words, one syllable to a word.

The others ask: "What is your hink pink?"

The player replies with a definition—that it is a fat fish. Then the group is supposed to guess that this particular hink pink is a "stout trout." If he is thinking about smart boys, the answer might be "wise guys." A skillful larceny would be a "deft theft."

After several hink pinks have been batted about, the game switches to Hinky Pinky, calling for rhyming words of two syllables. For example, a skinny animal would be a "bony pony;" a world of stone would be a "granite planet."

Hinketty Pinketty, involving words of three syllables, and lengthier variations are generally restricted to players with IQs of 150 and up.

YOU'RE IN

How to detect an imposter is taught here in a series of brief, easy lessons. A leader takes on the role of impersonator. She relates a capsule biography of a famous man or woman like this:

"I know I'm a great wit ... (pause for questions) ... I used to have red hair ... and later grew a white beard ... I associate with people of the theatre." The biographer, in this case, is boasting as would George Bernard Shaw in speaking of himself. But, to keep everyone guessing, she uses such devices as speaking in the first person, thus disguising the sex of the famous person, and she uses the present tense even if the famous person is dead.

The audience may ask the biographer questions, which should be guarded and indirect (not "Are you Shaw?") because those who are "warm" will not want to give away their hunch to the rest. Everyone in the audience is competing against everyone else!

A typical question would be: "Did you ever have a spouse?" which asks about "husband" or "wife" before you know whether the famous person is male or female. In the Shaw example, a player who is almost certain he knows would ask: "Did you ever have dealings with Cleopatra?" The biographer, realizing this questioner knows she is impersonating Shaw, will answer: "You're in." Another player, thinking of the white beard and forgetting the red hair clue, might hint at Monte Woolley in a question. The leader would answer: "No, you're not in."

The players "not in" keep up their bombardment until they are. Then the play begins over again with the first to be "in" doing the impersonation.

MUSIC DETECTIVE

Give your guests' musical memory some exercise that will set them to singing little ditties to themselves. You can play this game as individual contestants or in teams.

The game starts with the host playing several chopped-up bars of music on his stereo. Of course, he has prepared the music in advance, so he knows exactly what he wants to play. He may play:

"Hey hey hey, that's what I say."

"So c'mon and bring your jukebox money."

"You just call out my name ...."

Hurriedly, the guests jot down the names of the songs as closely as they can recall or guess. If in teams, the guests may collaborate and come up with one answer only. Naturally, at the end of the record-playing, the guest or team submitting the most correct answers wins.

An especially fiendish host will select strictly instrumental music, thus eliminating such essential clues as lyrics.

20 QUESTIONS

In this game one player thinks of something that is either an animal, vegetable or mineral. After she has decided what it will be, she asks the group of players to guess what it is. Knowing that there are only 20 questions in which to guess the correct answer, the players should be very selective in their questions.

The game can be made easy or difficult depending upon the experience of the participants. Besides using actual animals, vegetables or minerals, the objects to be guessed can be even remotely derived from the three categories. For example, penicillin made from bread mold can be traced to grain or plant life which is vegetable. Other examples are hot water bottle (vegetable), skiis (vegetable), Grant's Tomb (mineral), and a mink coat (animal).

For a start, a player announces to the group that she has an object in mind—mineral. (She alone knows she is thinking of the Rock of Gibraltar.)

The following questions might be asked, to which she answers "yes" or "no": The players keep count of the number of questions. 1. Is it in this country? *No.* 2. Can it be seen by the naked eye? *Yes.* 3. Is it above ground? *Yes.* 4. Is it valuable? *Yes.* 5. Is it big enough to be walked on? *Yes.* 6. Is it big enough for many people to walk on? *Yes.* 7. Do people live on it? *Yes.* 8. Is it in the eastern hemisphere? *Yes.* 9. Is it in Switzerland? *No.* 10. Is it Mt. Everest? *No.* 11. Is this mineral a symbol of strength? *Yes.* 12. Is it the Rock of Gibraltar? *Yes.*

5. Party Ideas

SEVENTIES PARTY

If you would like to hold a party that is different, a party with a purpose, theme or idea, try a Seventies party.

Dudes can come in bell bottoms, sideburns, and unbuttoned shirts. Chicks can wear hot pants or trouser suits with platform shoes.

The enterprising host and hostess should put up a disco ball and stock up on '70s music and drinks, such as Tab and Tang.

The feature attraction may be a disco dance-off, with the winner getting the soundtrack to *Saturday Night Fever*.

CRIME DOESN'T PAY

Everybody—young or old—likes to play "cops and robbers." You and your guests can release your repressed desires at a Crime Party.

Have your guests masquerade as pickpockets, gun molls, chain gang convicts, Sherlock Holmes, Charlie Chan, assassins, racketeers (flashily dressed), policewomen, shoplifters, panhandlers, jail matrons and swindlers (with mustache). You might screen (or even frisk) guests as they enter, just to make sure they've been invited and aren't in their regular work clothes.

Featured acts at the party could include a homicide (see the game, Murder), a police lineup (see illustration), a fingerprinting, a parking fine window, a policy number drawing, a room with military maps (so spies can steal them) and a shopping counter where shoplifters can operate.

A mock trial is lots of fun, with a judge, defendant, district attorney, defense attorney, witnesses and jurors. You can get confessions like "How I stole a crayon in kindergarten," and "Why my father gave me my first licking."

Musical atmosphere can be achieved with songs about prison, such as "Jailhouse Rock." Of course, for refreshments, bread and water will do—at least for a starter.

An enterprising host will hang rolls of black paper on the walls to simulate prison stripes. Other "props" might include a chair with wires for an electric chair. Breakable objects around the room should be replaced with rubber hoses and copies of detective stories and *Crime and Punishment.*

At the close of the evening, you might "parole" your guests with the requirement that each of them pose first for two photographs—one of the usual type and the other a profile. After putting a "Wanted" label on each photo with a convict number below, mail or email the photos later to your guests as a reminder of their evening in jail.

FUND-RAISER

Raising funds for a community service project is a noble avocation, but it isn't necessary to go about it in the manner of a tax collector. You can make it a pleasure instead of a chore by giving a Fund-Raiser party. Here are several ways, all popular, to make your guests vie for the opportunity to contribute to charity (tax deductible).

- Take several bottles with necks of varying sizes, such as milk and pop bottles, and stand them on the floor. Sell your guests 10 toothpicks or matchsticks for a dollar or whatever amount you want. Guests stand over the bottles—no bending allowed—and try to drop the toothpicks into the bottles. Anyone who gets a toothpick into a wide-necked bottle gets half his money back. Those who get a toothpick into a narrow-necked bottle get the jackpot—all their money back.

- Put a man's hat on the floor and deal out a deck of cards, 10 to a person. Charge a dollar or two for each card. Whoever flips all his cards into the hat from a distance of 10 or 15 feet gets his money back.

- Fill a pail almost to the brim with water and place it on the floor. Float a small ashtray or a jar lid on the surface. Guests try to pitch quarters into the tray from a position 10 feet away. Quarters that land in the water go to the fund, while those landing in the tray are returned. A scorekeeper may count the number of hits and award a prize at the end of the contest. Note to the host: have several rolls of quarters at hand so you can make change.

- If you can stand the wear and tear, set up a row of lighted candles and let your guests try to douse the flame with a water pistol at a dollar a squirt.

- Darts or other games—including many in this book—may be adapted for fund-raising purposes.

If the police raiding squad appears at your door, invite them in. News of the "raid" may serve as excellent publicity for your affair, and you should also see to it that the officers don't get away before buying some toothpicks and flipping a few cards and pennies.

HOLLYWOOD TALENT PARTY

The story, probably apocryphal, is that this party originated in Hollywood at a time when there was an excess of talent and little chance to show it off except at house parties. Be that as it may, this party gives all your friends a chance to show their special abilities. Certainly everyone has some special ability and can perform without previous experience. Don't look now, but your talent is showing!

Make sure to tell your guests to be prepared to present a brief act, song, story, joke, anecdote, musical composition, reading, pantomime—anything amusing or enjoyable.

When the guests arrive (in costume or not), be sure to establish a relaxed atmosphere, free of competition, so that each performer feels comfortable when performing. The sequence of acts can be determined by the hostess or by the guests volunteering, or by both methods. If someone in the crowd has a video recorder, make certain he brings it along so the acts can be played back to the guests at the end of the party or at a subsequent event.

SMALL-FRY PARTY

Why act your age? A Small-Fry party is an adequate substitute for the Fountain of Youth that Ponce de León sought for years, only to come back older than he started.

At a Small-Fry party, instead of *looking* for your youth, you bring your childhood with you. You arrive in the clothes you wore in first grade—or a reasonable facsimile thereof. You may borrow your child's or nephew's clothes or any part of their outfits, even just a hat. You can even make or purchase a costume.

The simple songs you will sing in chorus at the party will not tax even a monotone. You may sing "Ring Around the Rosy" or "The Itsy Bitsy Spider."

For an accompaniment, ask your guests to raid their children's toy chests for toy pianos, sets of chimes and other instruments to make up a "Small-Fry Orchestra."

For refreshments you can stage a mock birthday party for any guest who is still able to blow out five candles at once! Serve ice cream and soda pop with straws. Have bubblegum for souvenirs!

An old-fashioned spelling bee, crayon drawing and finger painting would bring some classroom education into the party, but don't introduce too much education. Your guests, fearing report cards, might raise their hands and leave the room.

COME AS YOU ARE!

Invitations to a Come As You Are! party *must* be made by telephone. Phone each guest individually well in advance. In case you're inviting couples, you must speak to both people, preferably at different times of the day.

The first thing you ask the guest over the phone is "How are you dressed now?" When he or she tells you, you say: "Come as you are!"

If the guest is in a robe—then that's it! If a man is in a T-shirt and shorts, he comes as he is. If a woman is wearing pj's and slippers, she comes that way.

When your assorted guests arrive on the appointed evening, you will undoubtedly find them in different moods to match their raiment. This should give your party a real lift. Of course the conversation of the evening will focus on what each was doing when the invitation came through. You will probably be able to play active games because of the informal dress.

ROARING TWENTIES PARTY

Almost a necessity for this type of party is a supply of hip flasks. You can sit around a speakeasy table with a checkered tablecloth—by candlelight, of course.

You'll want to do the Charleston so be sure to have the appropriate music. Perhaps a Black Bottom contest would be in order. Or you might prefer to hear the songs of the era, strummed by your amateur band of ragtimers on mandolins and ukuleles.

If you can find them, screen some of the old silent films starring Doug Fairbanks, Mary Pickford, Noah Beery, Charlie Chaplin, Charles Ray, or Tom Mix.

Men should come dressed in tails or a dapper suit, and the women will have their best flapper hats and dresses to display.

The conversation will naturally tend to stocks and bonds, to that financier who jumped from his office window after the market crash, to debates on "keeping cool with Coolidge," stories of Will Rogers, and the Lindbergh solo flight across the Atlantic. The more you know about the era, the better the party is going to be.

PICNIC

Those of us who don't mind an army or two of ants frequently go to picnics. Community, office, factory and family picnics are a wonderful institution, and we here note a few ideas that ought to make them at least as enjoyable for you as for the ants.

Besides some games selected from the outdoors chapter of this book, you should stage a few "contests" giving prizes for each of the following:

- Youngest boy present.
- Youngest girl present.
- Couple married longest.
- Boy or girl with most freckles.
- Guessing number of beans in a jar.
- Guessing distances, such as number of feet between two points in front of judging area.
- Person who can throw a softball or volleyball the farthest.

And don't forget to top it all off with either a softball game, square or social dance, or a campfire sing-along.

AUCTION BOX LUNCH PARTY

To raise funds for a cause, try an Auction Lunch.

Every guest brings a box lunch. It is generally a good idea to agree beforehand how elaborate or simple the lunch should be. Each box should be giftwrapped, as one factor at the auction will be the gaiety and originality of the wrapping.

In looking for an auctioneer, remember that they are made, not born. Anyone can serve. If you have more than 15 guests, you may need two or three auctioneers.

Each box is auctioned off—at a limited fee or with Mars the limit, whichever course has been agreed upon. The only universal rule is that guests may not buy their own lunches.

Each lunch should be a surprise, a pleasant surprise. So if you have packed a peanut butter and jelly sandwich when turkey and prime ribs of beef have been declared the order of the day, you should leave your surprise at home!

Pass the bicarb—I mean the salt—and keep your comments to yourself!

6. Dramatic Games

IN THE MANNER OF THE ADVERB

To start on the road to dramatic fame, "adverbial" acting is excellent practice, and entertaining at the same time.

One of the guests is chosen "It" and leaves the room, while the others agree on an adverb. When "It" returns, she tries to guess the adverb by asking one player after another to act it out in pantomime. For instance, she may say, "Eat in the manner of the adverb," in which case the guest must pretend to eat slowly if "slowly" is the chosen adverb. If unsuccessful in guessing, "It" may turn to another player and say, "Laugh in the manner of the adverb," and that guest will have to laugh slowly in pantomime.

"It" is entitled to ask one performance from each player. If she fails to guess by that time, she has to give up. The crowd tells her the adverb, and another adverb is chosen while "It" goes out again. Should "It" be successful the first time around, the player who gives away the adverb then becomes "It." If "It" names a synonym—leisurely for slowly, etc.—this is considered a correct guess.

Add zest to your game by using zesty adverbs, such as jerkily, lovingly, spontaneously, enthusiastically, industriously, alertly, conceitedly, and so on.

CHARADES

The ancient game of Charades (or The Game) is still as popular today as it was before the movies and television. Playing charades was considered good preparation for acting in the silent movies.

You've seen those wordless love scenes. The villain silently threatening the heroine. The inarticulate but comic cops. Have YOU ever tried acting that way? Charades is the game dedicated to the preservation of pantomime.

There are many variations of charades, but all have one element in common. A performer acts out—without talking, without writing, without touching any objects or otherwise using "props"—a word, phrase or idea for others to guess.

WORD CHARADES

A play in syllables.

Cast of Characters: James Smith, playing the lead, a silent role.
The nonguessers, who have written Smith's script. The audience, who tries to guess Smith's message.

SMITH holds up four fingers.

AUDIENCE: The word has four syllables.

SMITH holds up one finger.

AUDIENCE: He's going to act out the first syllable.

SMITH goes through the motion of pushing a lawn mower. Does it again and again.

ONE OF THE AUDIENCE: He's mowing the lawn. Mow?

SMITH nods head affirmatively, then holds up two fingers.

AUDIENCE: Now the second syllable.

SMITH pretends to be tying a knot near his shoelace without actually touching his shoe or lace.

ONE OF THE AUDIENCE: Knot? Not?

SMITH nods affirmatively again, indicating a right answer. Displays three fingers.

AUDIENCE: Now the third syllable. "Mow-not" so far.

SMITH pretends to sit down on a chair.

VARIOUS MEMBERS OF AUDIENCE: Chair? Sit? Down?

SMITH shakes his head negatively to all of these.

ONE OF THE AUDIENCE: On?

SMITH nods head affirmatively, then holds up four fingers.

AUDIENCE: "Mow-not-on" is what we have. Here's the fourth syllable.

SMITH points to everyone in the room with a wide gesture and includes himself.

AUDIENCE: Us! "Mow-not-on-us." Monotonous!

The Timekeeper (one of the non-guessing team) checks the time on his watch.

You have just witnessed a game of word charades, played with teams, in which Smith was acting out the word which the non-guessing team had made up. The length of time it took Smith's team to guess the word counts as his team's score. After Smith's performance one of the nonguessers picks a paper slip with a word on it from Smith's team's box. Now *she* must pantomime the word for his team, which becomes her audience. And so the game goes, with all members of each team having a turn. The lowest score, counted in minutes and seconds, wins.

If you have five or fewer players, it is better to have each person play individually, instead of in teams. In this case, each player makes up her own word. The score of each is kept and the player with the lowest score after several rounds is the winner.

If the audience cannot guess the charade within a certain time limit, the performer or her team receives the full time as its score. Three minutes is the usual limit for one word.

BIG-TIME CHARADES

After your group of silent thespians becomes adept at one-word charades, it is ready for the Big Time. These longer charades are played and scored on the same principles.

The mystery phrase may be a slogan, quotation, title of a song, book or play, proverb, TV show, movie, historical event, national or international activity, or anything that is a well-known combination of words. Each team gets together in private and decides what phrases to write on the slips and put into its box for the opposing team to dramatize. Usually a limit of eight words to a phrase is agreed upon. The length of time for guessing, when using an eight-word limit, is generally five or six minutes.

In the Big Time, the teams are allowed to use standard signals, which are decided upon and announced in advance, to denote conjunctions, articles and other minor words, such as "and," "the," "of," "from," "to," "although," and so forth. Many players signal by holding up thumb and forefinger about one-half inch apart; others touch the top of their heads with one finger; some hold up a crooked forefinger. Whatever you choose, the signals may also be used if a syllable of a long word sounds like a minor word, such as "on" in "monotonous," which Smith may have denoted with a signal in the previous charade, instead of sitting "on" a chair. To show that your problem phrase is a quotation or a title, you may hold up two crooked forefingers to resemble quotation marks.

Big Time is played like Word Charades, with a player from one team picking a slip from the other team's box. He gets a minute to study the phrase and decide how he is going to portray it. He may decide to act out the whole idea in one grand fling, in which case he sweeps his arm in a big circle to show this is what he will attempt. Otherwise he begins (when the timing starts) by holding up as many fingers as he has words to act out. Then he holds up fingers to indicate the word of the phrase he is starting with, for example, three fingers to show he is starting with the third word. Now he holds fingers across the raised palm of his other hand to indicate the number of syllables of that word, and finally he shows fingers across palm to indicate the syllable he will begin with. He acts this out and goes on to the next word or syllable. If his team has difficulty guessing, he may decide to go on before they solve it, or choose another way of acting the same thing.

The performer usually chooses to give the minor words first, using signals, so his team only has to fill in the blanks. He can wave his team on if they are close to guessing, but haven't hit the spot exactly.

Nonguessers have just as much fun as guessers if they don't peek at the slip the performer chose. His acting is likely to be just as puzzling to them as to his team.

Here are some easy phrases that will serve as starters: "Show me the money," "I wanna hold your hand," "Give me liberty or give me death!" and "The DaVinci Code." Sometimes a team will guess the whole phrase correctly if it gets one word, so the performers must try to hit upon the key word first. For instance, if he poses with one arm raised like the Statue of Liberty, his team will quickly get Liberty and from this it is but a short step to Patrick Henry's famous words.

Here's a hint for making up tough phrases: the hardest things to dramatize are intangibles, concepts and words of value, such as "free." You are not allowed to use "props" of any sort in dramatizing and you can't draw letters or signs in the air either.

Ready? Camera! Lights! Action!

ART CHARADES

Pantomime is fine for most of the evening, but after several hours of gesticulating and grimacing your guests may become jittery. Before tedium sets in, switch to art charades.

In this type, the ideas are represented on paper in pictures or diagrams, rather than acted out. First the group is divided into equal teams. The nonparticipating host whispers a title, slogan or word to one representative of each team simultaneously. The players then rush back to their assembled teams, take up paper and pencil and try hurriedly to illustrate the given idea to their team. Teams may not peek at the other's art.

Any symbol may be used in the drawing but words and letters of the alphabet cannot, of course, be written out. For example, if the idea to be drawn is "New York City," one "artist" may draw a skyscraper silhouette, while the other may sketch a series of theatre marquees.

One point is awarded to the team guessing the charade first. Each player has a chance to try his hand at sketching, and then the team scores are tallied to determine the final winner. Save your sheets of paper after you are through, and compare them with the art that your children bring home from kindergarten.

MUSICAL CHARADES

Having trained your cast in one-word and multiple-word charades, you are ready to play the musical variety of charades. Here all the crowd, even the "extras," get into the act but, since pantomime is preserved, you will not hear voices. Instead of singing songs, one troupe or team acts out one or more of the song's verses for the other team to guess. It is probably just as well that the game is silent.

You should dramatize the idea of the song rather than its individual words and syllables. For instance, "Yankee Doodle Dandy" may best be done with the whole team marching and saluting. "On Broadway" may be done by mimicking a line of chorus dancers. "Jack and Diane" can be acted out easily.

If a charade proves too difficult for the audience to guess, the acting team may generously drop a hint as to what type of song it is—whether jazz, rock, classical, or pop.

Musical charades are less competitive than the other types, but definitely just as amusing.

MAKE ME LAUGH

Poker players should be excluded from this game on the grounds of greater experience and superior willpower. After the game is over, all the guests may attend the coronation of the Mr. and Mrs. Sourpuss of the party.

Starting off, the guests sit in a circle and watch the antics of one volunteer (usually the host or hostess) who is "It." "It" stands in the center and does everything she can to make the audience laugh. She may stick out her tongue, tell a joke, laugh herself, sing a song, do a dance or ape one of the other guests. Anything goes, but all holds are barred—meaning any touching or tickling of the guests.

The audience, of course, tries to refrain from laughing. When one does laugh, he must step into the center of the circle and join the horseplay. Finally, the center area will include everybody but the two champions.

PAPER BAG DRAMATICS

You don't have to be a dramatist to play this game. All you need is a paper bag full of assorted items and a good imagination.

Here's how it goes: Divide the group into teams with about five to 10 players on each team. Then take several paper bags—one for each team—and fill them, but put different objects in each bag. Then each team has 10 minutes to prepare a skit using the objects in the bag.

For example, Team A has a bag containing a banana peel, a comb, a lady's purse, detective's badge, a mustache and a handkerchief. The group may decide to enact a skit that can go like this:

Two underworld characters, one with a mustache, are planning a robbery. They are sitting on a park bench, and the thug with the mustache is eating a banana. He takes the banana peel, rubs off his fingerprints with a handkerchief, and tosses it on the ground (not on the rug, please) for an unsuspecting victim to slip on. A woman with a purse walks along, slips on the peel. One of the thugs comes to her rescue, and helps her get up. As she opens her purse to take out a comb to rearrange her dishevelled hair, the other character darts out and grabs her purse.

She and the first thug run after the robber, but he escapes. A detective appears wearing the badge. He sees the banana peel, and upon examining it finds a hair on it. "Aha," he wisely proclaims, "the man who was eating this had a mustache." Our thug quickly pulls a razor out of his pocket and begins to shave off the mustache, but he is caught in time, etc.

Don't bother to memorize lines, just make them up as you go along. You'll be surprised at your hidden talent.

SHADOW PLAY

False eyelashes, eye shadow, and makeup are not necessary for this play. It's your shadow that counts.

First thing you'll need is a sheet. Hang it in a double doorway or on a clothesline stretched across the room. About six or eight feet behind the sheet place a lamp or a spotlight if you have one.

Once you've set up the sheet and light, turn off all the lights except the one backstage behind the sheet. All action takes place between the light and the sheet. You will notice that the shadow will be much larger than the actor. Take advantage of this by using equipment that makes humorous or interesting shadows. And, be sure to practice just where to stand in relation to the light and sheet.

For your shadow play you can use all sorts of devices. You can have one or more actors do pantomimes while others speak the lines or use simple narrations. Remember it's the shadow that counts, so make use of it.

One play that can be done is a surgery scene. The patient lies on a table, and the doctor removes the intestines, pulling an endlessly long rope from the vicinity of the patient's abdomen. Another player might complain of a pain in his nose. As he talks to the doctor about it, the nose gets larger and larger. This can be a balloon that the patient blows as he describes his symptoms. The doctor can slowly move a pin toward the bulbous nose until he eliminates the difficulty with a bang!

Just let your imagination go for good shadow plays, and have fun!

7. Games for Large Groups

APPLESAUCE

There are perhaps 101 ways to eat an apple, but here is the easiest way: Become the "anchor man" on a team-of-five when Applesauce is being played.

The hostess gives each team an apple and a paring knife. The first player on each team peels the apple. Second player cuts it in halves and the third player slices the apple into quarters. No. 4 removes the core from each quarter. Then No. 5 eats the apple! First to finish wins, but don't eat so fast that the apple brings the doctor instead of keeping him away!

You can play Applesauce with more than five on a team simply by adding another process—such as slicing the apple into eighths—for each additional player.

WARMER UPPER

(This is an all-around mixer, excellent to start off a mass activity with 20 people or more. It provides 10 minutes of group activity during which your guests will get warmed up and set for other games or activities in your program.)

You begin with "Simon Says." If you are leading this game, take a prominent position facing the group and have the players stand about eight feet apart so they will have enough space for free movement. You begin by saying, "Simon says, hello," and everyone must then say hello.

Next you might say, "Simon says hands up." You raise your hands and everybody follows suit. Then if you say, "Raise your right leg," and you raise your leg, the players must not obey the command, because it wasn't prefaced with "Simon says." You can make the game very funny by purposely confusing the players. For example, you can say, "Simon says, hands on hips," and at the same time you place your hands on your head. People will be amused when they find themselves doing what you *did*, rather than what you *said*.

As players make mistakes, they drop out of the game and form a line to one side. You can continue playing till only one player (the winner) remains; if the game goes on too long and seems to pall, you can stop.

Now you lead the line in a game of "Follow the Leader." If you are the athletic type, don't make it too strenuous for the others to enjoy. Walk around the room in a figure "8" and then turn and walk sideways a few steps, try a hop or two, a skip and a jump and a few minutes of a simple exercise. The idea is to leave the guests refreshed, not exhausted, and all sparked up for the rest of the festivities.

PASS THE ORANGE

This game has met with its greatest success at parties before guests become bored with the usual exertions: talking, eating and sitting. Since it teaches how to keep your chin tucked in, perhaps it was originally designed for prize-fighters with "glass jaws." It never fails to win laughs and sometimes develops a contortionist or two.

Start by dividing your group into equal teams, males and females, alternating if possible. The idea is to pass an ordinary orange from one member of your team to the next, right down the line, using your chin alone. You'll be surprised how useful that part of your anatomy can be when you are prohibited from using your hands.

Each leader (the first in line) tucks the orange under her chin. Next person must remove the orange with his own chin and be ready to surrender it to a third chin. First team to pass the orange down the whole line wins.

If the orange falls to the floor, the player with the clumsy chin must pick it up with her chin. This is a game that not only breaks the ice but gets your guests intimately acquainted very rapidly.

OPPOSITES

If you happen to have an extraordinarily large number of guests, try Opposites. As a substitute for formal introductions, this game has met with unparalleled success.

Pieces of string of equal size are handed to each guest, and then all the guests gather in a circle. In the center of the ring stands the host or hostess, holding the other end of each string. The formation resembles a wheel, with the guests forming the rim and the strings like spokes. The "wheel" rotates as each guest in order calls out his or her name. Everybody must listen carefully and particularly try to remember the name of the person on his or her right.

Now the fun begins as the host shouts commands. Each guest must answer each command by doing the *opposite*. Not only that, but each guest must imagine he is not himself, but the player to his right. For instance, when the leader says: "All first names from A to M, drop strings," each player must go through a lightning reasoning routine like this:

"I'm the person on my right. His name is John (I think). So I'm John now. The leader said all first names from A to M, so I'm in that group. What am I supposed to do? The opposite of what he ordered. He said my group is to drop strings so I'll hold on to mine."

Sounds simple? Suppose the person on your right is named Ralph. Then you would be not an "A-to-M" name, and you would have to drop your string, because you must do the opposite of what the leader commands, and you must respond to each order. As the host barks out a variety of commands, in progressively faster order, he usually gets these results:

- His guests catch on fast and have riotous fun.
- They learn each other's names because they switch identities (especially if you make position changes in the circle).
- They forget their own names. This is a signal that it's time to start another game.

SPARE A DOLLAR

Is there anything that will spur a large party to get acquainted? Yes, a few dollars! Politicians have been known to shake hands with their enemies for just a vote. For a dollar reward, most people will shake hands with anybody—unless someone knows of another house party where fives are being passed out!

The hostess subtly extends her bribe by making it part of a game. Secretly, she gives dollars to a few confederates, choosing one confederate for every 5 or 10 guests. Then she announces that a *few people* in the room are holding dollars and that their money will be given to the lucky 5th, 10th and 15th guest to shake the hand of each.

Well, whose hand would *you* shake? Not knowing who has the dollars, you won't be likely to take any chances. You'll shake hands with everybody! Meanwhile, as the campaigning progresses, the confederates keep count of the guests who greet them. After everyone's hand has been through the wringer a few times, Santa's little helpers make themselves known and give out the dollars to the winners.

Now that everybody's acquainted, let them keep the change—it was worth it!

BUZZ

ANNOUNCER: And now, Mrs. Burlingame, will you please tell the audience how old you are?
MRS. BURLINGAME: Buzz-buzz.

• • •

WIFE: Were you gambling again? How much did you lose?
HUSBAND: Rags-bones.

• • •

These are just two examples of how useful the language of Buzz can be, and how, once learned, it can save you from embarrassing situations. But, to buzz or not to buzz is not the question. The real issues are: when to buzz (answer: it's wonderful fun while you are riding or waiting) and how to buzz (see below).

Buzz is a counting game. Let's say that you have chosen 3 as the buzz number. The first player counts "1," the second player "2" and the third player must say "buzz" now instead of "3." The counting continues, going in a clockwise circle, "4," "5," "buzz" (since 6 is a multiple of 3). The next buzzes come on the numbers 9, 12, 13 (since 13 contains a 3), 15, 18, 21, 23, 24, etc. When the count reaches the 30s, the correct forms are: buzz (for 30), buzz-1, buzz-2, buzz-buzz, buzz-4, buzz-5, buzz-buzz, buzz-7, and so on.

Players are eliminated when they say the number instead of "buzz" or when they say "buzz" for the wrong number. The game continues without them and the last player left in the counting wins.

The game is often played with 7 as the buzz number. You can actually use any number or any number of buzz numbers. For instance, you may have 3 as "buzz" with 5 as "rags" and 7 as "bones." Under these conditions, the count in the 50s would sound like this: rags (for 50), buzz (for 51), rags-2, rags-buzz, buzz, rags-rags, bones (for 56), rags-bones, etc.

As a parlor game with a large crowd, try Super-Buzz. The object is for the crowd to count to 100 without an error, using 3 for buzz, but having the direction of the count switch from clockwise to counterclockwise every time a player says "buzz." Even a convention of mathematicians would have trouble with this.

ALPHABET RACE

We adults, at party after party, speak with piteous longing of our childhood days, passing, such remarks as: "I wish I were back in fifth grade and really living again!" Let's not kid ourselves. What were we doing in fifth grade? We got report cards and we had spelling bees. Nothing too difficult about holding a spelling bee. In fact, we will find that spelling is a wonderful pastime for adults, provided that two or more heads are put together and we can see that all our friends are in the same class. We may even get rid of our spelling complexes by this reversion to childhood.

This is the way to do it. A leader (host or hostess) writes certain letters of the alphabet, one each, on the backs of a number of paper plates or on 5 x 7 pieces of cardboard. She writes the same letters once in red crayon and once in black crayon on two sets of plates, making one plate for every person in the group. She should use an abundance of vowels use letters like "H" and "K" sparingly, and perhaps give out no "Q"s or "Z"s. The leader should also have a list of words prepared in advance using only the letters on the plates.

The game starts with the guests dividing into two equal teams. One team gets the plates with red letters and the other the black.

Each team now has exactly the same letters. When the leader calls out a word (for example, "Arbitrary") the players on each team holding those letters rush to opposite ends of the room and hold up their plates to form the word—correctly spelled, of course. First team to form the word correctly scores a point. Then the teams come back to the center and are ready for the next word.

Although a large guest list allows for the more difficult and longer words to be formed, Alphabet Race is equally successful with small groups. The leader may call out a simple word, such as "Camp." Immediately several "A"s from each team rush to their goal. There is only room for one and they may cause their team to lose a point. With a very small group, two or three letters can be given to each player—and then watch the fun!

If your guests turn out to be good spellers and find the game too easy, you can keep them winded by calling out the names in quick succession. Or, you can keep them punch-drunk with false leads by calling out the key word at the end of a long, involved sentence recited slowly, such as: "On the advice of party stalwarts in Congress, the President avoided a fight over tariff revision, although he endorsed the reciprocal trade agreement, which had been described as, on the whole, ARBITRARY!" Then watch them run!

BOOK RACE

There is only one way books can meet competition from television—the book must be made indispensable. Therefore, we offer this game which can be played much more easily with a book than with a television set.

Give a book (each about the same size) to each guest. Have the players face a line on the other side of the room or about 20 feet ahead. Let them balance the books on their heads. Then, at a starting signal, the players race toward the distant line, reach it, turn around and race back. Hands may be used only after a book slides off a player's skull and hits the ground. Before that player again moves forward, he must pick up the book and balance it on his head, then drop his hands to his sides. The winner is the player who makes the round trip fastest.

In larger groups, it's a good idea to play the game as a relay, with one book being given to each team. When a player returns to the starting line in the relay, he hands the book to the next racer, and so on, repeating the operation, until one team wins.

For a super-duper race, use dictionaries or encyclopedias.

NUMBERS

Numbers is designed for those occasions when host and hostess consider groups of one practically illegal. It keeps everyone hopping, gabbing and making friends.

The hostess's job is to sound off in the proper manner. When she barks, "Mix into threes!" the guests scurry into groups of three. Then quickly the hostess-sergeant shouts: "Mix into fives!" The guests stumble over each other in order to get into groups of the required size. You will find that at some point your guests become too excited to count straight.

Conversation comes naturally under these circumstances. Keep on calling until all the guests meet each other. Of course, any hostess who leaves her guests panting too hard will be defeating her purpose.

SALTY WHISTLE RACE

The art of whistling has lost its nobility and sunk to unspeakable depths—i.e., the wolf whistle. In this game, we will attempt to revive the art through constructive channels. Every home has salty crackers. Each guest should be given one. The purpose of the game is to whistle as soon as possible after eating the cracker.

Give a starting signal and let all your guests get a fair start.

The last player to whistle receives a penalty. He must whistle an entire song. If you are thinking at this point—what's so hard about whistling after eating a salty cracker?—try it yourself.

HUMAN BINGO

If you don't know Bingo by now, it's time you learned this new way.

First, each player is given a sheet of typewriter-size paper (5 x 7) and also a small slip of paper on which she writes her name. Than the host collects all the name slips in a small box, counts them and announces how many players there are. Upon learning this number, each player takes his big sheet of paper and draws a chart of squares on it. (See diagram on the facing page.) If there are 9 to 15 players, she draws 3 squares in each direction, making a total of 9 squares; if there are 16 to 24, he draws 4 squares horizontally and vertically, giving a total of 16; if there are 25 to 35 players, 5 squares each way, making a total of 25; if 36 or more players, use a chart with 6 each way, with total of 36.

Now, each player takes her chart and walks around the room, asking names and writing them down in the squares in any order she prefers. However, she must write a *different* player's name in each square, and when she has completed her chart it should be filled. (She may not have some players' names on it—as, for instance, with 19 players she will have only 16 squares with names.)

When the charts are ready, the host reaches into the box and pulls out one slip at a time, calling out the name on the slip. The players then put an X through that name on their chart, if they have the name. When one player (or more) has a complete string of crossed-out names on her chart in a straight line, either horizontally, vertically or diagonally, she shouts "Bingo!"

For a second play-off, the slips of paper are all placed in the box again, new charts are made out and the same procedure is repeated.

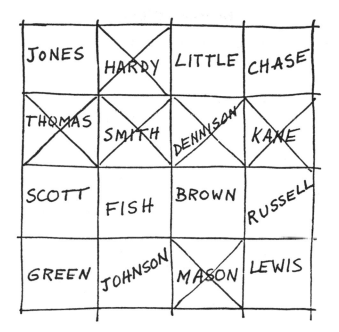

On your Human Bingo chart, a straight line of Xs in any direction is what you are aiming for.

CARRIER PIGEON RELAY

In this game, everybody gets a chance to flap his wings and act like a homing pigeon. First, the host provides all the guests with makeshift beaks in the form of paper or plastic soda straws. He also divides the group into equal teams and gives the leader of each team a "message," which is really a piece of paper no more than two inches square. Flight is achieved by flapping arms as you run, all the while clenching your straw between your teeth and holding the paper at the other end of the straw by sucking in your breath.

As the game gets under way, the leader of each team must run to a line across the room (or about 20 feet away), keeping the paper on his straw without use of hands. If the paper should drop, he must pick it up by inhaling on the straw.

When he returns from across the room, he delivers the message to the next player in line, who must then do the same thing. And so on, until each player has been a pigeon. The first team to complete the flight wins.

8. Picnic and Outdoor Games

SHOE SCRAMBLE

To release the frustrations of those who have never been able to push their way through crowds at a bargain counter and grab the article in demand, this game is just right. Try it with a big crowd at your next picnic, indoors or out.

All the players must take off their shoes to play. Then all the shoes are mixed up in one big pile on the ground or at one end of the room. Equal teams are formed, and a starting point is set at a good distance from the pile. At a signal, the first player on each team dashes to the pile, finds his own shoes, puts them on and returns to his team to tag off the next player. First team to graduate completely from the barefoot state wins.

If the players are few (or even if you have a big crowd), the game may be played without teams and with all the players racing for the pile at the same time. This more closely resembles a department store scene. Expert shoppers need not bar themselves from the game, but should refrain from crowding after they succeed in finding their bootery.

MINT RELAY

An approach to the problem of how to use the hole in a doughnut is made in the Mint Relay. Use small candy mints with center holes (one for each team) or if you prefer, play the game just as successfully with doughnuts and sticks.

First, organize several teams of equal number and have them line up in single file. Arm each player with a toothpick, and give each of the leaders a mint. The leader spears the mint with her toothpick in her mouth, turns and tries to pass it to the toothpick of the next player. No hands allowed.

When the mint has been passed down the line, toothpick to toothpick, and reaches the last player, that player runs with toothpick and mint to the head of the line where she assumes the first position in her file. Everybody moves back a step. The mint is passed again. Each of the players must carry the mint, and the first team to finish the whole sequence wins.

If the mint should fall from the toothpick, it must be picked up with the toothpick alone—with no hands allowed. You'll find toothpicks are somewhat fragile and can't withstand much pressure.

THREE-LEGGED RACE

To play this game, just imagine that you and your partner are making a break from a chain gang. You are standing side by side and your adjoining legs are tied together with a soft rope or rag. This combination of limbs is what is known as the Third Leg.

Now all the three-leggers line up in teams. The first pair of each team is going to make a break for it, as the cheering section lets loose. The racers run, hop and jump to a wall or line 50 feet away, then back to the starting line. After they tag off the next pairs, they are allowed to roll on the ground exhausted. The spotlight stays on the race as the pairs each get a turn to run. First team to "escape" completely wins.

With a small group, all the three-leggers can race at the same time, but must avoid bumping the pair in the adjoining lane.

CIRCLE LEAPFROG

While the steaks are being broiled over the charcoal, or when the tide is out and the sand looks inviting, here is the ideal game to build up an appetite without going anywhere. It's like a merry-go-round.

Divide your group into equal teams, with each team forming a separate circle. The players should stand front to back and an arm's length away from each other. Then each bends over, placing his hands on his knees.

At a signal, the leader of each team begins to leapfrog over his charges. When he completes his round and returns to his original spot, he taps the player in front of him, who then takes off in like fashion. First team to finish stands erect with all of its members panting in unison. The prize may be an extra steak for each of the heroes.

SUITCASE MYSTERY

Getting dressed and undressed at a picnic in front of an audience may sound shocking to Aunt Matilda, but just let her play too and she'll see why people have such fun playing Suitcase Mystery.

Begin by dividing the group into several equal teams, assigning a suitcase to each team. If the teams each consist of five players, for example, you would then place five pieces of clothing in each suitcase, in other words one item for each player. Use both male and female items of outer- and underclothing. Then put the suitcases about 50 feet from the starting line.

At a signal, the first player of each team runs to her team's suitcase, opens it, clads herself in the *first* item of clothing she touches (be it a second pair of underpants or a necktie), closes the suitcase and dashes back to her team to tag off the next player.

As soon as everybody on the team has donned one piece of clothing, the game continues in reverse without stop. The first player races off again to the suitcase, opens it, takes off the item of clothing, puts it in the suitcase, closes the suitcase and runs back to tag off the next player. First team to finish wins.

You will see some unusual outfits, but nothing likely to set a new style.

BLIND HORSE TURNABOUT

Here is a grand opportunity for each guest to turn the tables and become a backseat driver temporarily. Divide the group into couples—male and female pairs preferably. One of each couple puts a paper bag over his or her head (becoming a "blind horse") and the other becomes a "rider" or backseat driver.

A straightaway course of about 50 feet should be selected. Then all the teams of horses and riders line up at the starting line. The riders act as guides, orally directing the horses but never touching them after the turnabout at the start. At the signal, the horses are turned around by their riders three times. Dizzy or not, off they then go on the trail with the riders urging them: "Whoa! Right! Bear left!"

When a pair completes the excursion in one direction, the horses remove their paper bags and become backseat drivers, and the riders become horses. Back the horses come down the homestretch, after being turned around three times by their riders. The first team to complete the course wins, and has the right to claim backseat honors.

SALUJEE

If there were a glossary in this book, almost everyone would look up the word "Salujee," which would be defined as follows:

Salujee is an outdoor (or indoor) game played with a knotted towel (sometimes with a rubber ball or baseball). One of the players ("It") must catch the towel. The other players, formed in a circle, throw the towel to each other, keeping it from falling into "It"s hands. If "It" intercepts the towel in midair, he changes places with the person who made the throw, and that player becomes "It." However, "It" may also seize the towel while it is in a player's hands—not only when it is being thrown. The player responsible then becomes "It."

In lieu of a pass across the circle, a short lateral may be made to an adjoining player. This generally fools "It." Another method is to feint a throw. Teasing "It" is acceptable—a player may hold out the towel and as "It" draws near throws it over his head. Sometimes the player may hold the towel too long and "It" will yank it from his hand or block the throw. This is as good as an interception.

In other words, Salujee is similar to a passing drill in basketball practice and it can be just as strenuous.

CRAB AND MONKEY RELAY

Walking is okay, but too much of it gets tiresome, even if you're not in the infantry. Imagine all the miles you walk, walk, walk—just from the kitchen to the living room, and from home to office.

Is there no relief? The answer is yes. People are capable of getting about as the crabs and monkeys do, effortlessly.

To walk like a crab, use all fours, with your back parallel to the ground. Steer with your feet, and let your hands bring up the rear.

To walk like a monkey (and feel like one), bend forward, place your hands on the ground in front of you and proceed on all fours. You'll wobble just like an ape.

At your next outdoor party, divide your guests into equal teams and have the teams line up single file. The first player in each line must walk like a crab to a line 30 feet away, and return walking like a monkey. They tag off the next players in line and the relay keeps going the same way.

After a number of relays, you'll find that walking around the house like a crab or monkey is a relaxing departure from your usual routine. (Don't try to explain your actions to your children.)

DODGEBALL

There's nothing like that old favorite, Dodgeball, to raise a sweat—and an appetite for wieners, ants and even sand.

Divide up into two teams. One team forms a circle and the other team stands within the circle. The players of the outer team have a volleyball or beach ball that they throw at the center players in an attempt to eliminate them. A toss of the ball, a touch on the ankle, foot or leg and the touched player retires from the game. The circle team may toss the ball around the circle in an effort to confuse their opponents and keep them on the run. The center players take a tip from the title of the game and *dodge!*

A timekeeper notes how long it takes before ALL the players on the inner team are eliminated. Then the teams change places. The group that survives longest inside the circle is the winner.

ELBOW TAG

Some people need a psychiatrist in order to learn when to make attachments and particularly when to give them up. Elbow Tag will teach you to do it—and fast—for free!

Divide your group into couples, not necessarily mixed. Let each pair link elbows and place loose hands on hips. Spot the couples about 15 feet apart. "A" and "B," an unattached couple, must find attachments.

"A" is chasing "B" and in order to avoid being tagged the latter decides to make an attachment. As he weaves in and out among the couples, he hooks onto a loose elbow of any other player, "C." Thus a chain reaction sets in. At this point "C"s partner, "D," must quickly detach himself and start running, for now *he* has become "A"s quarry.

When "A" succeeds in tagging someone the tables are turned. "A" becomes the quarry and he is pursued by the person he tagged.

ICE CUBE SURPRISE

Nothing is so refreshing on a hot day as an ice cube. It is usually found in a glass—floating on top of an appropriate liquid—but for the purpose of this game any plain fresh ice cube will do.

Half of the fun of this game is making the ice cube cometh as a surprise to your guests. So, first divide your group into teams and line up each team in a single file. Give table knives to the last person in each file. Then announce that everyone must keep eyes closed as you hand an object to the first in each line. The object is to be passed from player to player down the line to the rear person, who must put the object on the blade of her knife and walk (but not run) to a line 25 feet to the rear. On reaching there, she must turn around, walk back, pass the knife and object to the next player, and so on. First team to complete the relay wins.

When the object turns out to be an ice cube, the players will be so startled by its cold slipperiness as it's placed in their hands, they will be likely to drop it. Of course, this loses time for the team, as the cube must be picked up (with eyes still closed) and the passing resumed.

Eyes may be opened once the ice cube has reached the first anchor person and she starts with the knife. Practice with a cube on a knife and see how it handles. It slides but can be handled easily. Limit each team to five players or your ice cubes will disappear before the game is over.

9. Games While Traveling

NEIGHBORS

So long as the driver of the car keeps on the road and is not confused when he hears the names of other states, it's all right to play Neighbors.

One passenger takes the road map and says: "I am Kansas. Who are my neighbors?" The others try to name all the states bordering on Kansas, and the player naming the greatest number of them inherits the map. He names another state, asking for *its* neighbors.

After you cover the United States and learn anew its 50 contiguous states and their locations, you can enlarge your scope to "Good Neighbors," which concerns Latin America. Then go on to the map of Europe, Asia, etc. It's best to have an up-to-date atlas in the car.

EPPIZOOTICS

Ever since Abraham Lincoln wrote the first draft of the Gettysburg Address on the back of an envelope while riding in a train, people have been trying to devise an equally good way of utilizing such wasted space. Eppizootics leads the way!

Two or more "authors" may gather in conference. Each of them draws on the paper in preparation for the game 25 squares, five boxes across and five down. The first person calls out a letter—for example, "P." He and the others must write a "P" in one of the squares. The next player calls out a letter; and each in turn calls out until 25 letters have been announced. All the players must write down each letter before the next is announced. There is no restriction on the letters to use, and they may be repeated more than once in the group of 25.

Each player, as the letters are called, tries to arrange them within his squares in such a way as to cause them to spell out a maximum number of words, horizontally and vertically, the maximum being 10 5-letter words. Proper nouns do not count. Scoring is 10 points for a 5-letter word, 5 points for a 4-letter word and 3 points for a 3-letter word.

For example, one row may contain s-p-a-r-e. This is a 5-letter word for which the player gets 10 points. Any other words occurring within one already counted (in this case, p-a-r-e) are not counted.

No juggling of letters is permitted. For instance, if you have s-e-p-a-r and you want to erase and change them, you cannot. If your row contains a letter in the middle that breaks up a sequence, the word cannot count either. For instance, if you have h-x-a-r-e, you cannot count it as "hare" but only count the "are" as a 3-letter word. If you had h-p-a-r-e, you would count "pare" as a 4-letter word. If you have s-u-n-a-p, you count either "sun" or "nap" but not both.

If you are given a letter that you cannot manage to work into the words you are trying to form, you have to put it down anyway, wherever you think it is later going to do the most good. Score is kept for a series of games, and the winner is crowned King or Queen of Eppizootics.

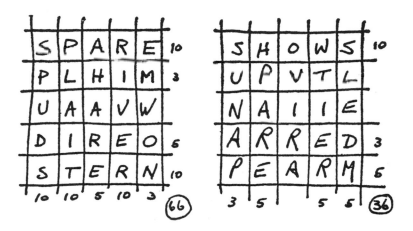

The same letters can give you 66 points—or 36!

MAGIC FIFTEEN

When it comes to making travel pleasant and speedy, high-compression engines run a close second to the game of Magic Fifteen.

Supply your players with pencils and give each one a sheet of paper with nine blank squares (three-by-three). The squares are to be filled with the numbers from one to nine, no number being used twice.

Here's the trick: the numbers must add up to 15 in all directions—horizontally in all three rows, vertically in all three rows, as well as the two diagonals. Try it yourself before peeking at the solution, which is hidden away in the back of this book!

Most of the players will spend a long time at it before admitting that they can't figure it out—after all, the permutations and combinations are almost infinite—but anyone who does work out the solution should be permitted to stand all hands to a round of soda pop.

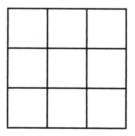

Solution on page 126.

MATCHING WORDS

One reason for having two eyes is to be able to see everything in one-and-two combinations, to know what goes with what and who with whom. For instance, with Adam we usually associate Eve. With "before" (in an advertisement) we generally find "after." Get it?

With pencil goes paper. Take pencil and paper and you can play this game anywhere with two people or more. One player is the leader and has a long list. The leader calls out A.F.L. (You write C.I.O.) She says Laurel. (You write Hardy.) Abbott (Costello). Democrats (Republicans). B.C. (A.D.) Minneapolis (St. Paul). Tom (Katie). House of Lords (House of Commons). Brother (Sister). And so on.

The leader should call off the names in rapid-fire order. The winner of each round is the player whose list most closely resembles the leaders. If only two are playing, a 90% average of correct matches wins. As his reward, the winner gets ham and eggs, bread and butter, or his hat and coat—whichever combination is voted him by the losers.

LANDMARK ADDITION

Automobile and train trips will seem as fast as spaceship travel if you eat up the miles playing Landmark Addition.

To begin the game, draw up a list of the objects you are likely to see, taking into consideration the part of the country you are in. For instance, you assign a higher point value to an Eskimo if you happen to be in Alabama, than you would while driving through Alaska. The player who first sights the object gets the points.

Here is a sample scale of points:

Horses (one, a pair, a herd) . . .2	Golfer 4
Red light 1	Lightning rod 2
Railroad semaphore 2	Lake, pond or river 1
Freight train 2	Motor boat or row boat 2
Red barn 1	Fisherman 3
Farmer in field 2	Pheasant, duck or turkey . . .4
Farmer in field with plow 4	Hay wagon 5
Cyclist 3	Deer 6

Winner is the player who gets the highest score in a 25- or 35-mile stretch.

ALPHABET BILLBOARDS

After you have covered the first 50 miles in the car and your conversation begins to show signs of ennui, it's time for a commercial. Radio and television commercials help to break the continuity, to say nothing of the monotony. The highway commercials take the form of billboards.

You read the commercials on the billboards and adapt them for use in Alphabet Billboards, a game that requires no knowledge of advertised products—only some familiarity with the alphabet.

Contestants may be two individuals or two teams. Each of you looks for the first phrase on the billboards that contains an "A"—like "Stop! Eat at Joe's!" Each player writes it down and circles the "A." Next, you try to find a phrase containing a "B." The first player (or team) to complete the alphabet wins. If you spot a phrase containing two desired letters *in order*, such as the "D" and "E" in "Hotel DEarborn," you may copy that word and circle both letters.

We strongly advise the driver to stay out of the game while driving!

GEOGRAPHY

Here's a way to enjoy travel: *play* Geography.

One player begins by naming a city, like "Chicago." The next player must answer with the name of any city, state, or country beginning with the last letter of the previous area named, in this case, "O." Let's say we choose "Oklahoma." The rejoinder to that could be "Australia." No name can be used more than once. That's what makes it difficult.

The game goes on and on, with everybody answering in turn. When a player is unable to think of a name beginning with the last letter of the one just given, he must drop out. The last person left wins.

Sometimes a time limit is imposed on each player. The limit is measured by having everybody clap hands 10 times. As in prizefighting, on the count of 10, you're out!

HOW'S YOUR VOCABULARY?

You've tested your vocabulary many times, but have you ever staked your word-knowledge against that of your friends?

Try this game on yourself and your guests. Give everyone pencil and paper and provide yourself with a watch that has a second hand. Announce a letter of the alphabet and allow 60 seconds for everyone to write down as many words as possible beginning with that letter. Each word they list must have three or more letters and must not be a proper noun. Plurals and different tenses of the same word don't count. If you're an average person, you ought to get off 15 words in a minute.

Easy letters to start them off on are A, B, E, G, H, N, O, S and T. More difficult are J, K, Q, V, X, Y and Z. The player with the longest correct list wins.

MY TRIP

Please do not take this game seriously. It is not true that people only *air Airedales in Alaska, bake biscuits in Belgium, can codfish in Canada,* or *dance daringly in Denmark*. If you qualify your gossip by remembering that you are playing My Trip, which is only a game, then everything will be all right and our ambassadors will not have to apologize.

While the car continues on its way, one passenger will say: "I'm taking a trip to Alaska. What will I do there?" The second passenger must answer with a verb and a noun beginning with the same letter as the name of the place, *"address advertisements in Alaska."* After answering, Passenger No. 2 will pose a similar question, referring to an area whose name begins with "B" for example, "I'm taking a trip to Brazil." Passenger No. 3 answers and then "throws a "C" to No. 4. When a player fails to answer on three occasions, with a reasonable time elapsing after each question, she is ruled out of the game. The winner is the last player left.

By this time the car has reached its destination and everybody gets out to wash windows in Wyoming, if that's where you were headed.

PARTY PLANNER

Date: _____

Guests: _____

_____

_____

_____

Theme: _____

Decorations: _____

Menu: _____

_____

_____

Games Played: _____

_____

_____

PARTY PLANNER

Date: _____

Guests: _____

_____

_____

_____

Theme: _____

Decorations: _____

Menu: _____

_____

_____

Games Played: _____

_____

_____

PARTY PLANNER

Date: _____

Guests: _____

_____

_____

_____

Theme: _____

Decorations: _____

Menu: _____

_____

_____

Games Played: _____

_____

_____

PARTY PLANNER

Date: _____

Guests: _____

_____

_____

_____

Theme: _____

Decorations: _____

Menu: _____

_____

_____

Games Played: _____

_____

_____

PARTY PLANNER

Date: _____

Guests: _____

_____

_____

_____

Theme: _____

Decorations: _____

Menu: _____

_____

_____

Games Played: _____

_____

_____

PARTY PLANNER

Date: _____

Guests: _____

_____

_____

_____

Theme: _____

Decorations: _____

Menu: _____

_____

_____

Games Played: _____

_____

_____

PARTY PLANNER

Date: _____

Guests: _____

_____

_____

_____

Theme: _____

Decorations: _____

Menu: _____

_____

_____

Games Played: _____

_____

_____

PARTY PLANNER

Date: _____

Guests: _____

_____

_____

_____

Theme: _____

Decorations: _____

Menu: _____

_____

_____

Games Played: _____

_____

_____

PARTY PLANNER

Date: _____

Guests: _____

_____

_____

_____

Theme: _____

Decorations: _____

Menu: _____

_____

_____

Games Played: _____

_____

_____

PARTY PLANNER

Date: _____

Guests: _____

_____

_____

_____

Theme: _____

Decorations: _____

Menu: _____

_____

_____

Games Played: _____

_____

_____

Index

SOLUTION OF MAGIC FIFTEEN

2	9	4
7	5	3
6	1	8